Eglosow Kernow
Cornish Church Poems

by
Donald R. Rawe

LODENEK PRESS

First published by Lodenek Press 2005

© text and illustrations: Donald R. Rawe 2005

© cover illustrations: Carol Williams 2005

ISBN 0 946143 29 3

Typeset by Able Graphics, Totnes

Printed by Eden Print Ltd,
Treleigh Industrial Estate, Redruth, Cornwall TR16 4AX

Published by Lodenek Press,
1 Fernleigh Cottages, Probus TR2 4PY, Cornwall
Tel. 01726 883564

Contents

For Jennifer

Acknowledgements

Most of these poems have appeared in various magazines and publications, including Cornish Review, Cornish Scene, Cornwall Today, Cornish Banner, Abraxas, Old Cornwall, Katholic Kernow, Quaker Monthly, St Petroc's Magazine, Padstow Echo, Roseland Magazine, St Minver Link, Poetry Now, and the anthologies Cornish Links and The Dreamt Sea. Due thanks are made to the respective editors and publishers. I wish also to thank Maggie Sams Quintrell for help with calligraphy, and Pat Munn (Bard Trevenson) for an illustration.

D.R.R.

Preface

Cornish churches have always had their own very significant place in our consciousness. They are landmarks, repositories of history, and witnesses to the enduring faith of the people. Many, like St Ervan, Lanlivery and Advent, have been allowed to decay, but have recently been repaired and renovated by immense public effort aided by Heritage funds. That they have been so lovingly restored is proof of the determination of those who worship in and visit them that these temples of the spirit shall survive intact into the future.

There have been several high water marks of ecclesiastical building in Cornwall, as in Great Britain generally. One was during Celtic times, when the saints (so many of whom actually founded our churches) arrived from Ireland, Wales and Brittany to convert the native Cornish and Dumnonians to Christianity. Almost nothing survives of these buildings (St Piran's Oratory-Chapel, buried under the sands at Perranporth, is the main exception); but the legends and great deeds of those missionaries, most of whom predate Augustine's landing in Kent by at least sixty years, survive in our hearts and minds to this day.

A second great building period took place during the 'Norman' period, about 1100 to 1250, when stout cruciform churches with towers over the crossings were built of local stone across this western land. St Anthony in Roseland and St Hilary, though both much restored, give us an idea of the form these churches took. Tintagel church, with its thick walls and narrow windows, best suggests their atmosphere.

By the fifteenth century these Norman churches had deteriorated, and many were too small to accommodate a growing population of worshippers. The Great Rebuild of that century, drawing finances from the tin and wool trades, and the contributions of pilgrims journeying through Cornwall to reach the Shrine of St James at Santiago in north-west Spain, gave us the extent and shape of most parish churches as we know them today. Anchorite cells, like the one at Roche Rock, were built and inhabited during that period.

A further wave of church building came in the nineteenth century, when most of our parish churches were restored – and new edifices of various denominations rose to serve expanding towns and villages.

Our churches have undergone various periods of neglect and vandalism: one such was during the seventeenth century, with Roundhead cavalry often stabled in them, and granite crosses and stained glass windows, as well as statues and icons, wilfully destroyed. Neglect during the Georgian Age brought the need for restorations, during which too many medieval screens and carved bench-ends were thrown out and burnt, and wall paintings covered up. The decline in church attendance during the twentieth century left many places of worship poverty-stricken, damp, cold and uninviting.

All this has changed. Some churches have been declared redundant, though even among those, as at St Anthony in Roseland, repair has been effected. Many Methodist and other nonconformist buildings have been closed and sold for other purposes. But others, along with Anglican and Catholic premises, have been much improved over the last twenty years or so. Much of this is due to the injection of interest and money from new arrivals in Cornwall, who have moved here to work or to retire, and a dedicated nucleus of local Cornish people have steadfastly striven to keep their churches and chapels in use and healthy repair. Funds from government Heritage bodies, the Historical Churches Trust and other charitable organisations have greatly helped.

I believe it is important that everyone, and especially newcomers to Cornwall, learn something of the history and tradition of this very significant heritage. For what would Cornwall be like without its churches? Surely not even the most sceptical agnostic would wish to contemplate such a scene. So much of the spiritual richness of this Little Land (as Dr A. L. Rowse used to call it) would be lost. For even now, in this era of profit-making, pleasure and materialism, most of us are baptised in a church, married in a church, prayed for in a church if we are ill, and given our funeral rites in a church, whether of Anglican, Catholic, Methodist or some other persuasion. We might well pause to wonder why this is so, since church-going is now so unfashionable. Could it be because at the back of our minds, in the depths of our souls, we know that the church is our mother, the handmaiden of God, the Bride of Christ, and that in times of trouble and extremity – but also of relief and thanksgiving – she and her cherished buildings will always be there for us?

These poems, I hope, will prompt some of us to reflect further on such questions, and to value (or revalue) the rich and varied legacy our forebears have left us in their places of worship.

D.R.R

Homage to Sir John Betjeman at St Enodoc

He lies beneath a slab of Delabole
Ornately scrolled, his name alone inscribed:
'John Betjeman, 1906 to 1984'.
Beyond the graveyard, surf comes tumbling in
On Daymer Bay, just as he used to see:
Thongweed on the foreshore, entwining plastic cans
And bits of nylon netting, orange, electric blue.
He knew it and foresaw it all,
Each piece of flotsam from our wasteful world,
Each relic of the ocean's wrath. Yet loved
The trembling thrift, the bright foam on the sands
Dying before the sea wind off Pentire,
This simple stalwart church, this western cell.
Blessed St Enodoc, pray for us all,
For young and old alike, the lusty and infirm,
For businessmen on golfing holidays,
And fading Poet Laureates struck down with Parkinson's.

Sir John, who once wore one brown shoe
And one black at the country outing of his firm,
Who pedalled as a youth along our lanes
Discovering in the hawthorns mildewed shrines,
Refurbishing them in prose and poetry,
Opened our eyes to what we'd held in scorn.
'Padstow has a fine slate harbourside,
Also a hideous Post Office – red brick.'
He rinsed from me those cheap and tawdry views,
The hollow brash aesthetics of our age,
And brought me back to saner, quieter things.

The tamarisks along the hedge now sing
And feather-dust the salty air that flows
Up Sinking Neddy's twisted spire, beyond
To Himalaya bunker and the sixteenth tee

7

Below Brea House within its copse of pines,
And Jesus Well in suppurated turf
Deep-plashed by bovine hooves this wild wet March.
At Wadebridge they are raising further cash
To build a Centre worthy of his name;
But here, for me and you the poetry breaks out –
In every organ note and Celtic cross,
From all the slates of this once buried church
(Where couples used to climb down through the roof
To pledge their marriage vows inside).
Summoned by the eternal bells of heaven,
Chasing new bats in belfries marvellous,
Tending new lights in chancels well restored
On planes sublime, now free from palsied stress:
We bless his memory here, who saw so well
These riches which he loved and left to us.

The John Betjeman Centre for Senior Citizens has been developed from the
former railway station buildings described in *Summoned by Bells*, Betjeman's verse
autobiography.

The Angels of St Endellion

The angels of Endellion have seen so much,
Staring down from wall plates above the aisles and nave:
The tomb chest of the saint herself, carved in Cataclewse,
Wherein her bones were kept, mouldering into the Middle Ages
Until the Reformation banished or dispersed them;
The Master of Endellion and his workmen, sculpturing
This masterpiece of masterpieces, blow by blow,
Stroke by caring stroke, until the elvan glowed
With subtle pearly sheen, as evening sun
Or candlelight picked out the noble tracery.
Nicholas Roscarrock, who compiled his 'British Saints'
In prison, worshipped here; his Hymn
To that fair lady saint, alas, was never heard
In those fierce times of terror.

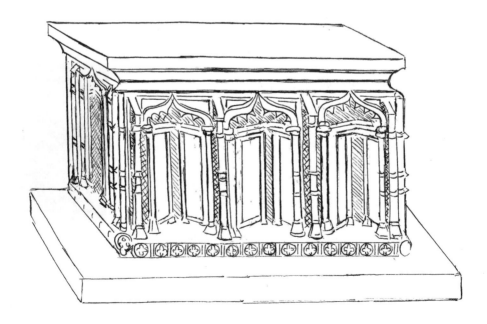

                    Here the Squires
And farmers of Trelights in high box pews
Snored through their Rector's dusty sermons. Deaths
And burials, births and christenings, weddings, women churched,
And Easter celebrated down the centuries
With daffodils and primroses in jugs;
Paupers and the nameless worthies all consigned
Along with Samuel Billing, William and Mary Cole,
Adolphus Trevan of Camelford, and William Bate,
Lost with the barque Lord Riversdale at sea,
Digory and Elizabeth Ward – though these impose here yet
Their names on grave and ponderous marble plaques
Upon these rough cast concrete-rendered walls.
The slender granite piers and capitals march on,
A silent elegant procession, down the years
To us who sit and contemplate another world:
The realm of music these had never heard.

What might an angel, stiffly carved in oak,
Make of Poulenc and de Falla, rhythms furious,
Outrageous, syncopated horns and clarinets,
Cascading harp notes of Ravel, the smouldering
Soprano bodying forth in passion
Gipsy flounce, flamenco and fiesta?

Mozart's Requiem, Bach's St Matthew Passion,
The glories of Tallis, Purcell or Palestrina
They might well understand. But wooden faces,
Plump, ascetic, grim or gracious, here betray
No preference, approval or disdain. The church
Is once again, as in the past, a meeting place,
A family centre where we may merry make
Or else commiserate among us for our lot:
And thus it was in distant medieval days.
The Rector offers up our thanks for music,

Greatest gift of God and his angelic choir.
The evening comes in wet and windy as we go
Into the stormy dark beneath umbrellas,
Sliding on the mud to find our cars.
A few remain to hear Compline. The angels stare
Down unsurprised at covered harp, the tomb
Chest littered now with books and scores,
The tubular bells and timpani that made
Such unimagined and amazing sounds within
The quiet shrine of this, their Celtic saint.

The Mermaid of Zennor

The thing to remember about mermaids is, they sing.
This one bewitched Mathy Trewhella, enticing
Him down beneath the waves. See, she's chanting
What wild and distant threnody we can only imagine,
Holding her comb and glass, but fixing us
With a cold indifferent eye.
                              Symbol of love,
Of power, of Christ himself; Aphrodite risen from the sea,
Isis the man-eater: take your pick. In Senara's church
She lures the tourist, folklore addicts, and children
Goggling at her nakedness and scales, carved
In medieval wood. Like her sisters at Seaton,
Cury and Padstow, she spells out doom, promising
Life on the ocean floor amid hermit crabs, congers
And drowned cathedrals.

Below the Logan Rock
The church, huddled with farm and pub and cottages,
Offers us moorstone memories, a rough Norman font
Restored, drowned sailors in the churchyard, and a sundial –
'The Glory of the World Passeth' (1737). In the former
Wesleyan chapel they're making furniture. Nothing much
For visitors here, beyond the Wayside Museum, a drink
At the inn, and of course the Mermaid: who still
Sings on her ageless chant, framed in a bench-end,
Crudely, luridly fashioned as if by the scrape of boulders,
The scouring of waves and currents. Siren,
Fish maid, sea lover, whelk-wombed water wench,
Big bellied gape-navelled tri-finned fury,
Of all God's creatures that ever might have been
Most magicked, mysterious, combining love and lust,
Spirit of shore and sea flesh mingling,
Casting her slithering spiny spell
With her endlessly swaying voluptuous song.

Echoes in Lanlivery Church

(written in 1980, before considerable restoration and refurbishment)

No one remarkable lies buried here:
None more famous than John Kay Kendall,
Major, R.A. – affectionately known as Dum Dum,
Writer of Light Verse. But all around
The stone-flagged aisles and gravel paths,
Remembered on brass plates or simple slate
Headstones, eaten and beaten by the upland wind,
Are personalities vibrant still
After centuries of dust. Here you may feel them,
Hear them speak, times even see them move
As the dimmits close in on autumn evenings
And the wind dies swirling and singing
About this elegant Caroline tower
With whirling weathercock and tapered pinnacles.
Stand in the south porch by the leaded glass –
Two diamond-shaped panes missing, needing varnish
(In Memoriam Charlotte May Atherton,
Relict of Robert Atherton, Vicar of Ratcliffe):
Regard the lifting grass and Celtic crosses
Where village forebears lie, guardians of more
Than their own memories, under the moving skies,
The constellations wheeling through the years,
Waiting for Judgment Day and Resurrection;
Dreaming perhaps of pipes and fireside chairs,
Beer in the inglenook, decades of toil
Upon these lonely farms, their marriage feasts,
Wrestling deeds and favourite songs,
Bell-ringing feats by their own team and by others
(Remember the old song: the Ringers of Egloshayle
Came here), their own beloved carols, viols and clarionettes,

14

The girls they had to marry, came to love,
Or shared with them a life of bickering strife
Till death did part, if only temporarily.
Sickness and disease they bore with fortitude,
Calling them the Will of God. No thoughts
Of suicide, no violent protestations:
      'Affliction for long time I bore
      Physicians were in vain
      Till God did please Death should me seize
      To ease me of my pain.'   Women's sighs
Mingle with the dying gusts, and bring
Thoughts of childbirth in those primitive days,
When every other son or daughter died
Before maturity. 'In parental love
To Jonathan Cecil Easterbrook of Breny,

15

Born November 6th 1874,
Died February 19th 1876.
Suffer the little children to come unto me.'
Under the wind-carved beech with branches all aligned
South-west to nor'east, by the little arch
With iron gate, and on the upper ground
That overlooks Lostwithiel and Fowey,
They bear insistent witness with their names:
Treleaven, Chapman, Rouse and Carne,
Kendall, Rundle, Verran, Lobb,
Beswetherick, Vague and Northey. Here's
Hugh Lyttleton, who died in 1740, leaving
'A widow and two hopeful daughters.' His family
Lived on; this year another Lyttleton, John,
Captain of the Tower, was laid to rest, aged forty-two.
Repeated here and there, the generations
Marching down the ever-present centuries:
Resigned to lose their quiet lives in soil
They knew so well, to gain a nebulous glory
Beyond this vale of tears ...

> 'Dear wife and child I must leave you
> Likewise relations dear
> Tis God's command for we to part
> And leave our friends so near.
> Tis like a watch in dead of night
> Time passing swift away:
> God summons me to my long home
> In this cold bed of clay.
> My feeble body come from dust
> And to the dust return.
> So as it is the Will of God
> Dear Friend I pray not mourn.'

And so they pass before our eyes, awaiting resurrection:
'Gone to Rest,' 'Laid to Sleep,' 'Departed this life' –
But not, O Lord, O sweet St Brevita,
Not dead! The earth attests with slate and rock,
Granite proclaims, marble and brass affirm
Their faith and hope, their unquestioning intention
To live a life beyond. And while they can be named
They still exist for us to know today,
Who by the canons of agnosticism think,
And after each cremation come to apprehend
That once dissolved or fierily consumed
We are annihilated and forgot by all
But one succeeding generation: who
May spare a while from pressures and neuroses,
Remembering our fading faces and our words.
(Then, nothing. So shall we be cast
Truly into outer darkness, a people lost,
With neither names nor epitaphs, except for those
Whose acts and speeches are recorded in
The local paper or on tenuous tape
In archives: sad substitutes
For a monumental headstone or a plaque.)

The Church too marches down the centuries,
Steps faltering here and there, dragged or quickening,
But conscious of its ministering tasks,
The focus of eternity and life, salvation, hope
And mundane welfare here. 'To the greater Glory of God
And in loving memory of Muriel Appleford
The electric light was installed into this church
By her daughter in 1955.' Lord, let there be light,
Electric and numinous, plasma of thy Spirit:
So let our people see from year to brighter year,
Moving to greater comforts, greater banes and griefs.

17

The hearty Vicar rallies now his flock
(Or some of them at least) with chatty news
Told on duplicated sheets at twopence each.
'We're facing a bill of £600 for the roof ! Next month
I'll tell you what we mean to do about it ...'
'You did well! The merry jumblers who jumbled £27 –
Big thanks to you all!' So he inspires his flock,
This minister who cares for every birth and death,
Enjoying all the social life and times
Of Lanlivery and Luxulyan. And they strive to keep
Their church in order, pleasant in His sight,
Who looks upon their every actions, every week,
With fatherly approval and allowance; so they hope.
Amid the paeans of material goods,
The praise of luxury and modern fads,
The urge to buy what these can never afford,
Self-seeking, violence, crass stupidity,
Blared at them from screen and radio,
This priest and his parishioners work and pray
To keep their place alive and reverent,
Their quiet lives devoted to content
On earth; the after-life they leave
To providence. They cultivate their farms and plots
And their own souls, regarding no man's scorn,
Nor envying those who come and go each year, –
Invaders of the clifflands and the shore,
Despoiling even such inland solitudes as theirs.
The granite tower soars up to heaven still,
And in its shadow they shall live in peace.

After the Storm

(On listening to the Padstow Carollers)

Now the storm has subsided
Hear the silence of the world.
Pause from the hectic motions of our times,
The ceaseless surge of human gain and grasp.
Neglect endeavour. Cast aside
The multitudinous small concerns that daily
Besiege us. Listen.

Now even the sea is dumb; the moors
Moan softly with the passage
Of ancient winds that burn them icily
Each winter, as in the days of Neolithic man.
(He never heard our desperate concatenations,
The complex orchestras of our torn desires,
Though his own drums still throb faintly in us.)
The ocean swings now, moving on the groundswell
Trawler and crabber and buoy-moored yacht
As it moved in far-off times
Trireme, coracle and hollow log canoe.
Thus the Romans and the maritime Veneti
Heard it: slowly quietening, a great sea-dragon
Satiated after its rampage.
　　　　　　　　　　　Listen:
Curlew plaints and oyster-catcher cries
Echo among empty rocks and caves.
Pines and fuchsias sway, minutely shivering.
Newborn December lambs cajole
Their placid dams, who shelter in the lew
From the unremitting blast of the dead nor'easter.
Now hark:
Carollers fill the air with glowing song:
Primitive harmonies rise and fall, interweave,

Fall briefly mute,
As bass or trebles hold the line alone.
Melody, innocent as Bible Christian faith,
Untrained voices in an eager burst
So nearly chaos, intuitively ordered,
Bearing devotion handed down generation
By generation, as my forebears sang
These self-same nonconforming part-songs –
'When the Youthful Son of Jesse' 'Rouse, Rouse
From Your Slumbers, Prepare a Glad Voice'
'Softly the Night is Sleeping On Bethlehem's Peaceful Hill ...'

At last then, having sung through winter streets
Of the grey town, by fairy lights and tinselled windows,
The glad sound fades and ceases.
Lambs call querulously. Waves rise and fall
In benediction on the moonless shore.
No birds cry. Listen.

Now hear the silence of the world.

A Quartet of Cornish Villages

(A pilgrimage in March)

In our aged mud-coloured Austin, letting in water,
We mapped a journey that easterly-burnt Sunday,
Our pilgrimage to the past, your quest for rural life.

I

Down swerving high-hedged lanes we reach St Kew
Where beeches lord barely over a mildewed manor house
And a cheerful pub keeps the old church company.
An Ogam-marked stone, a Cataclewse lantern-cross
Found by a former vicar buried in a leat;
One glorious Tudor window of red and purple glass
Recounts the Passion; the place redolent of monks
Who worked and worshipped here at Landocco
When Samson sailed up the Amble from Wales
To carve the first Cornish cross upon a phallic stone.
Kew, Docco's sister, stands queenly in Victorian glass,
A pre-Raphaelite virgin gracing the south aisle.

Outside the porch Elijah Wilce, a Master Mariner,
Sleeps under his marble anchor. Rook-haunted woods
Groan high above in the scything wind. A brisk walk,
Huddled and scarved against the blast; we seek the inn,
For jovial warmth and welcome whisky
Beside the Cornish range stoked full of split elm logs.
I pace the slate-flagged floor examining brass jugs,
Fox-tails and handbells, verse in praise of drink,
Hear the low hedge-accents drone, with bursts
Of rural laughter as the locals talk of pubs, beer,
Cars, and village choirs and bands: their soft and timeless
Aboriginal voices boom like bees, against the sharp
Wasp tones of Midland immigrants and Northern landlord.

21

In loving Memory
of ELIJAH WILCE
MASTER
MARINER
Born at St Kew 1840
Died at Truro 1924

Outside the naked trees stand waiting for the change:
The muddy farms, the fields with drifts of snow,
The foraging fieldfares and starlings shining mauve
In a sudden flush of sunlight, ask the sky
Can there be another season beyond the freeze,
A warmer world to burst upon these frigid lanes?

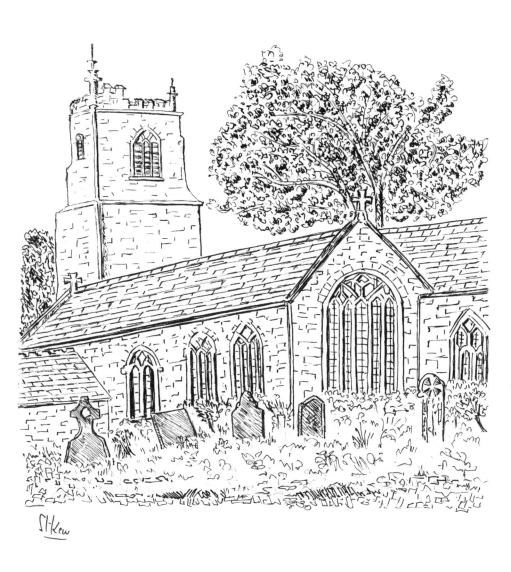

St Kew

II

By south and west we take the narrow road
To Highway: Ziglag Chapel (United Methodist, 1904)
Where David Watmough and his boyhood friends would sit
Still-faced, suppressing laughter as the preacher threatened hell
And dire damnation from the pulpit, whilst a captive lizard slid
From one boy to the other in the foremost row. Here shades
Of Wesley and O'Bryan call the faithful from their farms
And cottages, to raise to God hosannaed hymns
They cherish as a ground-bass to their lives.
'Come, Divine Immanuel, Come'; 'O for a Thousand Tongues to
                                                                    Sing',

And 'Love Divine, All Loves Excelling'. On we drive
Through dank woods of the Allen Valley, waiting
For the annual mists of bluebells to enrich their slopes;
And find, below the baleful fog-drenched moor,
The damp decay of mouldering Michaelstow.
O cold and clammy church, worm-eaten pews,
Scraped walls and plain-glass panes, cold-sweating floor,
Unvisited at this dead time of year: the squint
Through which the congregation watched the Host
Elevated, centuries ago, relates to us
Some semblance of that former age, high tide of faith
When Pope and priest and guild held sway
Over our simple unquestioning ancestors.
Tall oaks and beeches rock above the churchyard; now
The wind swings to the south-east, splattering rain
Coldly upon the slate and granite stones. The holy well,
Dry now for years, lies opposite the porch;
A single slender wheel-head cross, fifteen feet high,
Leans rakishly above the western steps. Slate cottages and farm
At Churchtown ring the village round, and woodbine,
Honeysuckle, vetch and campion
Lie lifeless, shrivelled in dry stalks and husks; yet roots
Stir deep within the hedge and verges, silently

Preparing for the Sun God's resurrection,
When Michael the Archangel shall attain again
The splendour he imposed on Hellesbury height
So many medieval days gone by.

Michaelstow

III

Past Hellesbury Fort to Helstone, crossing the main road
And by another chapel (Wesleyan, 1823) where cars
And lights within denote a Sunday Service,
And plunging down contorted lanes among
The sticks and switches, spikes of layered hedge,
Past sheep attended by their twitching lambs, we reach Lanteglos,
The old Church in the Valley: where
A Saxon stone put up by Aelnoth for his soul
Stands looking at three ancient Celtic crosses
(Probably eighth century). A light rain sprinkles us
Beneath the manor woods; the Georgian house appears
Half-screened by trees among its chalet complex,
And geese and Chinese ducks upon the pond
Gargle their cryptic comments. The church is locked;
Service today at Camelford itself.
                                        The neatly chiselled headstones rise
In ranks across the valley slope: Hocking, Keat and Best,
Kent, Trevethan, Sandry. I recall
That John Keats' father went from Cornwall, two centuries ago,
Finding work in Hampstead as an ostler.
The years roll back, these names resound along
The centuries, yeoman farmers, merchants, butchers,
Carpenters and smiths, millers, labourers;
Some still continue on the land their fathers worked
In those dim bygone times, through fat years and the lean.
A brief foretaste of spring now quickens in the air
As daffodils beneath the churchyard wall
Blow brave fanfares, returning light for light
To the returning sun, peering through clouds, the first
This sore afflicted year has seen.

Below the church the curved bridge crosses streams
In half-spate, bringing melted snow from Delabole.

Small buds prick out upon the sycamores and ash,
And now we watch a keening buzzard sail
Above the branching lacework, in a searing sky
Unruffled by the polar currents swirling there.
Along the earthbank hedge the hart's tongue fern,
The pennywort and flowerless foxglove leaf announce
Beneath the ivy's stranglehold, that sap will surge,
And from this deep and dark trough of the year
The urgent wave of springtime will arise.

IV

Placidly, primly Victorian upon the northern downs
Rises St Teath, a spacious city among villages
With elegant stone clocktower, its war memorial,
Church with turretted steeple and shining weathercock;
Rows of trim slate cottages, terraced houses,
Newly upholstered pub that boasts an open fire.
Arriving in a drizzle, turning to steady downpour,
We dash for the church, examine the barrel roof,
Carved screen (restored), a rector's effigy –
Thomas Coll, inducted 1450, who supervised
The rebuild of those times; the altar lit
By candles, and the warm and pungent smell
Of incense. Rich and noble, this,
The mother church of Delabole, commemorating captains,
Managers and overseers. Here all is slate,
The sustenance and profit of the district, worked
When Black Prince Edward was the Duke,
And still produced today, though not for common use.
An intricately carved memorial stands
To Frances Bennet, begowned with hat and cloak:
A well-born lady, with *memento mori*,
Skull and bones; buried October 1631.
> 'In life shee feared God,
> In death shee showed ye same.
> In life and death shee did Him praise
> And blest his holy Name.'
Out in the churchyard under slate slabs lie
Bawdens, Martyns, Nutes and Craddocks,
Tremaines, Brays, Harveys, spanning centuries:
Most of them marked by rude forewarning verse.
> 'O Reader now, whoe'er you be
> That read these lines concerning me,
> As God can quickly stop our breath
> Be sure prepare for sudden death.'

28

Snowdrops and crocuses spear through
The sodden green about the graves; tall cypresses
And mourning yews, a monkey puzzle higher than the tower
Compose this sombre and perpetual scene.
Beyond, the streets preserve the Sunday calm:
No one in sight, hardly a passing car,
Only the click of snooker balls where youths
Play in the ancient Parish Room beside the stepped
Lych gate. The rain increases, sweeping surely down
Against the wind.
                    Shall these dead arise,
Push up their coffin lids, thrust up
Like primroses and daffodils on Resurrection Day?
Will the living village resurrect

Into the stir of fellowship and trade?
No doubt a spring and summer will arrive
And with them tourists, trippers, and, like us,
Antiquarians of various kinds; St Teath awake
To unknown faces seeking petrol, cards, cream teas
And ploughman's lunches, pasties, scampi, steaks.
For three or four months summer shall hold sway
And commerce; then life will ebb to placid pace
And Women's Institutes and Buffs and dart teams meet
At Harvest Festival to celebrate the year's
Relapse to autumn and winter peace. The old
Look forward to their evenings by the fire; the young
Roar off on bikes and bangers down to Bodmin or Wadebridge;   .
And newly marrieds sit by twittering TV screens
Listening for the cries of infants short of sleep.

Yet all this is a process of slow time,
Eternity if you will: for humankind
Must like the seasons swell and grow and die;
Their only immortality, it may appear,
Lies carved on headstones, kept in parish chests,
In the legends of their lives recounted after death.
Upon their graves the frail snowdrops
And gracious celandines appear: above them rooks and thrushes
Nest; their pews are occupied by newcomers these days,
Though village life goes on amid the farming of the land
(One man where twenty worked a hundred years ago).

Change and rebirth in all around we see:
In life new deaths, in death more lives to come.
The clock strikes four, a dead despondent sound;
But up above, the whirling golden cock,
Caught in a break between the clouds,
Turns to a kinder quarter in a quickening shaft of sun.

The Windows of St Neot

No doubt they had such window panes elsewhere
Up and down Cornwall – probably at Bodmin,
Liskeard and Truro, the more prosperous towns
Where funds from tin and wool and other trades
Came to church coffers from parishioners
Who paid their tithes, and more, for their own souls.
But in the age of protest and outrage,
Reaction against such glorifying works,
Puritans, vandals, men of blind simplicity
Destroyed them for all time.
       Why St Neot
Was spared we merely can but guess. Too small,
Too far removed from moorland highways,
Hidden up the green Loveny vale? Perhaps.
At all events the works of Parson Tubbe,
Persuading his people, the landed families,
To raise to God in glimmering blazing glass
The stories often told, and played before
The villages and countryside at Corpus Christi,
Are still triumphant here – if delicately touched
In places by a kind restorer's hand.

There's more than medieval genius here:
Produced in leaded line, a sculptural art
Worthy of Gill or Epstein, flushed with wealth
Of colour – rich rose red and vivid blues,
Soft breathing greens and glowing passionate gold:
Actions freer, groupings more dramatic
Than in our modern or pre-Raphaelite effects.
Whoever drew and made these masterpieces
Loved their legends and their Bible lore:
For here's true social art, unsigned,
Mythic realisation of a living faith.

Neot himself, the fishes in his well,
The stags appearing to the brethren for the plough,
And Noah building his elaborate ark,
Setting forth the raven and the dove,
Sacrificing for deliverance, getting drunk:
Eve shyly takes the fatal apple here;
There Cain kills Abel in a bloody fight.
Christopher for Borlase, Christ crucified for Martyn,
St German and St Lallawy, with Tubbe himself;
St Mabyn and St Meubred, raised by parish wives:
All live for us today when sunlight glows,
Suffusing them with glory from the downs.

Such mathematics, wedded to true art,
Show the precision of the Creator's will:
Despite man's fierce rebellion and the evil sway,
God the Father, master architect of all,
Patient with dividers, rule and compasses,
Works his purpose out above the turmoil and the strife.

Sunday Afternoon Service at Lamorran

Storm-blasted woods by Ruan bridge
And lanes like rivers, bearing debris,
Torn branches, mud and leaf-mould: on this day,
The second Sunday in January, evensong
Is held, the monthly service at Lamorran church.

Small and gloomy, cruciform, it stands,
Cell of Saint Morenna, Virgin, abbess probably,
Beside the creek that joins the winding Fal
Under the high woods of Tregothnan. Almost
A redundant church; yet month by quiet month
A loyal congregation drives the miles
From Probus and Tresillian, hamlets round about,
Maintaining by devotion this relic of the past.
Here in the fold of valley, where September
Cyclamens in hundreds fire the turf with mauve
Among the graves of yeomen farmers and their wives,
The medieval cross without its head
Beside the porch, the isolated belfry, now disused,
We come together at Epiphany.

'We Three Kings' and 'As With Gladness' –
So the harmonium slocks us into voice,
Led by the cheery Truro vicar with his ringing tones,
Cajoling, almost bullying us to sing.
So dark the afternoon, the power being off,
We peer at tiny print by candlelight –
Yet greying tones outside still light Victorian glass
With heady blues and unreal reds. Beneath,
Against the transept wall, a carved slate slab
Records the deaths, and lives, of John and Catherine
Verman, he the squire and patron of this parish:
Died 1658 and 1666. They kneel,
Each in an arch with angel face above,

Prayer books in hands, in very piety. Nearby
A small slate limns their granddaughter,
Mary, aged three, died 1665.
                              These,
And the Norman font, present the glories of the church,
Though Betjeman points out (Shell Guide of '64)
The Georgian choirstalls and some medieval glass
Remaining in the transept.
                              After service
Young people gather by the Verman plaque:
'That was our aunt,' says one. 'How many
Greats ago was she?' – another. The worshippers
Depart for tea and biscuits at a nearby farm. The wind
Still blusters through the ashes, oaks and pines.
Slowly we wander up the lane. The church
Is locked up for another month, until
Another preacher comes, to bring to life
These simple stones and modest memories.

Parson Hawker Says Farewell

(Morwenstow, May 1875)

'From Padstow Point to Lundy Light
Is sailors' grave, by day and night.'

The sea-mist drives and drenches Vicarage Rocks
Where scores of corpses rolled upon the sands.
We brought them up four hundred feet, to lay
At rest in my beloved churchyard. Caledonia,
Brig Alonzo, Jeune Joseph, the Phoenix,
Primrose, Temperance and Nancy, Avonmore ...
The stench of rotting flesh would make us retch;
Fortified with brandy, our Christian duty done,
The County paid two pounds: the rest I had to find,
As when we built the valley bridge at Coombe
To span the weltering winter floods each year.
King William gave his bounty, twenty pounds:
Charlotte and I bore all the rest. 'Twas ever thus ...

Dearly beloved Charlotte, often then
My only congregation in this forgotten church:
No resident incumbent for so many years,
No vicarage, no school, and no community.
Moorwinstow I took, created Morwenstow:
And now they come, my vestry, labourers,
Farmers, wives and children, rich and poor;
Dissenters too, requesting burial.
(Delighted, I say, to bury all of you ...)
Ah, Charlotte, more my mother than my wife
They thought at Oxford ... Your great spirit led
And kindled me, sustained me in those years
When in my prime I strode the moorland ways,
Rescued those sailors, lit bonfires on the cliffs
As beacon warnings, gave the poor their Christmas
Fare, kept open house. And got in debt –
For who'd live here in gales and polar wind
Without a decent cellar for his comforting?

Disorientated, desolate when she died,
Smoking opium in my wreckwood hut,
I laboured at the 'Sangraal'. Tennyson
Came tramping down the coast, to stay and read
Those thundering lines, admire – and emulate.
His 'Idylls of the King' sells by the thousand still;
My epic, one shorn canto, torso of the whole
Masterpiece I planned, lies silent in the stores
Of publishers who, indolent, uncaring,
Make no effort with it. So it ever was:
Editors pay little, sometimes nothing. 'Footsteps'
Lingers on the bookshelves too. In London
I'd have been a literary lion; but how
Could I avoid that urgent call to serve
My far beleaguered Keltic station here,

Even in impoverished solitude?
　　'A house, a glebe, a pound a day,
　　A pleasant place to watch and pray:
　　Be true to church, be kind to poor,
　　O Minister ! for evermore.'
So once I thought; but then without a wife
And helpmeet I was cast into such gloom,
And should have done some dreadful thing perhaps
But for Pauline.
　　　　　　That God should bless again
And now with this young lively girl ! And I
Sixty years old and tiring of my cure,
Needing a woman's steady love to steer
Me through the shipwreck of my life !
My second marriage brought such joy, and three
Cherubic daughters, whom I fear to leave
In penury. For 'Children must be paid for,'
As on the omnibus. My dear Morwenna,
Rosalind, Juliot, will you live to see
The day you can forgive your ailing sire?

The church roof leaks. Oak shingles it must be,
But who's to pay for them? All here
Is dereliction, myself a drifting hulk:
My mind! It wavers like a helmless barque ...
The baleful grin of Arius yet mocks me in my shrine;
The devil rides abroad, in whirlwind and the storm,
But angels still glide up and down from Heaven
To bless our solitary paths. The waves of Galilee
Enfold the portals and the arch. Faithful
Must I be until mine end. I made this place,
This parish, from the waste, and it has worn me out,
Undone me ...

Tomorrow we depart for Boscastle,
Then Plymouth, to consult a Doctor Square. What quack
Of fortune, dancing on the fashion, will he prove? I can
Dispute and argue now no more. To leave this cell,
The chosen agony of my soul, the loveliest shore
And my Gethsemane, will be enough. Farewell –
I think I never shall return again.
                              My epitaph,
Which I must write out so that Pauline knows:
'I would not be forgotten in this land.'

At the Prophet's Chamber, Trewint

Here is the cameo that Burnard carved,
A boy aged thirteen, with his pocket knife;
This is the chamber built for those he loved
By Digory Isbell, seeker of the life
Everlasting, a son of Bodmin Moor.
They come here from across the globe, the Methodists
Remembering Wesley and his work among the poor,
The unheeded mass forgotten by the Church.

The wet wind howls, the clouds go swirling past:
In such a climate, riding through the mist,
The showers and thunder, bringing love of God,
The preachers came. And still is heard the Word
That spake through John and Charles and Billy Bray,
A hundred others who imparted self-respect
To tinners and farm labourers, bringing from neglect
The souls of fishermen and dairymaids and wives,
The drunken husbands who had terrorised their lives.
Simple their message, which the priests might have proclaimed:
Jesus' love is everyone's, high and low, they claimed:
All brothers, sisters, we in Christ: the Bishop and the Squire
As well as you and me, Mad Meg and Tom the Liar.
The Bishop and the Squire in general disapproved
Of these our half-starved people believing they were loved,
Exalted and transfigured by such doctrines they absorbed.
No matter: on the preachers went, the chapels rose on moors,
In villages and hamlets; the singing filled the towns;
A new wind, born in song, was swept across the downs.

    'Love Divine, all loves excelling,
    Joy of heaven to man come down:
    Make in us thy humble dwelling,
    All thy tender mercies crown ...'

Down the road at Altarnun the slate
Memorial on the former chapel guards
A memory more eternal than the plate
That Burnard chiselled. Faced towards
The Chamber in sober, kindly mood,
John Wesley watches still the friends he understood.

NN B 1836

St Hilary Revisited

They are still here, the well-loved images
And icons, gently presiding over the incense-
Filled atmosphere following High Mass.
Nine women, a man, three priests attend
(For this is Feasten Sunday – Hilary,
Bishop of Poitiers, died sixteen hundred years ago).
St Joseph proudly holds the infant Christ;
Simple St Anne, somewhat battered and wormy,
Broods over Cornish saints on painted stalls:
Morwenna, Endelienta's bier drawn by four cows,
And Piran preaching to the animals, his first
Cornish congregation.

Despite the schemes of past
Iconoclasts, they worship thus at Hilary,
As ancestors in medieval Latin did,
Before the English Prayer Book was imposed.
                                    Those Twenty Years
Were not misspent: the quiet saintly priest,
Courageous in his pacifism, harbouring refugees,
Rescuing slum children from their death in life;
Writing his Christmas play that sounded through the land,
Battling with consumption, friend of donkeys, miners, tramps,
Artists, men who husbanded the yielding land,
Revived here a tradition now unlikely to surcease.
Hail Mary, full of Grace ... *Sancta Hilary ora pro nobis,*
Agnus Dei qui tollis peccata mundi ...
Pray for the soul of Nicolo Bernard Walke
And Annie Walke, his dear beloved wife.
The slender spire that used to guide the ships

Sailing in with pilgrims to the Mount
Abides in silent witness to the love
Of these sequestered few, these members of the whole:
The sea of Catholic faith encircling all the globe.

'Twenty Years at St Hilary' by Bernard Walke is a Cornish classic.
Medieval pilgrims would disembark at St. Michael's Mount or Marazion after
their voyage to Santiago de Compostella.

Church Cove, Gunwalloe

Tidewrack on the shore by crumbling cliffs,
The debris of Mount's Bay continually washed up here:
Cans and plastic bottles, bits of fishing net,
Orange and electric blue, they lie among
The flatwrack and the thongweed glistening
In the sun's broadcast between the flying clouds.
Oystercatchers, turnstones and the little gulls
Probe among the flotsam; out beyond
Lancing down between the curling surf
Shags and cormorants ply their ancient search.
Huddled here behind its sandy hill
Winwalloe's church is sheltered from the blast:
A living church, where many printed sheets
Plead for charities beyond, abroad:
Shelter, Amnesty, an Indian Anglican retreat,
And Breton links are cherished here today,
Preserving fifteen hundred years of fellowship
Since Breiz and Kernow were one land, one family.

And dear eccentric Sandys Wason, poet, mystic,
Perpetual Curate of Cury with Gunwalloe,
Ultra High churchman – 'Everything is Mass to me' –
Is he remembered, eighty years beyond his deprivation, here?
The tamarisks sway and sweep the salty air;
The breakers in the bay still grumble in,
Eroding these soft cliffs, and flinging foam
Upon the churchyard walls and very graves.
The severed bell tower stands beyond the church,
And golfers drive the links below Poldhu;
Dominant flight of black-backed gulls,
Those butcher-birds; Mount's Bay beyond
And all the Atlantic surging at the door.
'O Lord, watch over me I pray:
Your ocean is so wide, my boat so small.'

We pay respects by writing in the book,
Contribute to church funds, and buy a card
(A simple drawing of the church amid its dunes);
And leave, refreshed and knowing why
This unpretentious shrine draws love and loyalty
From thousands more beyond its parish bounds.

Sandys Wason was once observed genuflecting before the stage at a London
theatre. When reminded that he was not at Mass he replied 'Everything is Mass to
me.' In 1918 he was deprived of the living at Cury for extreme High church
practices.

August at Mawnan Church

Mauve-fingered buddleia, mop-head electric blue
Hydrangeas, the shy white cyclamen too;
Graves bearing glowing heather and begonias;
Headstones of Mabe granite, crosses bearded
With grey-green lichen, by the two-stage tower:
Maunanus, Breton hermit, once kept vigil here,
With beacon fires to guide seafarers past this point.
Under the scudding clouds, between sharp showers
We sat on a churchyard seat to lunch:
'Gertrude May Coles, 1884 to 1978' – who will forgive us,
So we trust.
        Beyond, flotillas of white sails tack,
While clattering Culdrose helicopters pass above:
The Queen of the Fal barges downriver, full
Of trippers, from Helford. Here old 'Q' would sail
In peerless pre-War days, by Durgan to the sea...

St. Mawnan's church, a porchless edifice –
A drastic late Victorian restoration here –
Almost devoid, it seems, of parish life:
So few memorials within, no Sunday School nor Guild,
No notices of meetings or events,
Plain strait box pews, no stalls, no reredos;
No carved wood screen, no richly tinted glass;
Only the fine embroidery of kneelers
To whisper of devotion here today.
Only in the fluted granite of the piers,
The fifteenth century arcade, octagonal font,
A fragment of the replaced Jacobean roof –
Gilbertus Randall fecit, 1684 –
The list of rectors stretching back to far-
Off days of Tudors and the Angevins,
Something remains of history.
        But look outside:

45

There upon the tombstones one may read
The quiet tragedies and prides, the petty pomp
Of officers, devoted care of priests,
And those whose brief lives reappear for us
In glimpses of mortality on a slab.

Within a few days here died Emma James,
Aged four, and sister Eliza Jane as well,
But barely two: what epidemic snatched
Them from their grieving parents? Mary Ann Vosper,
'Sister, servant and kind friend, who lived
Thirty-two years with Mrs Pender' – who doubtless
Raised this stone for her. Emma, wife
Of Thomas Lawry: aged forty-four, she died
Leaving him, master of Tregarne, alone.
And Henry Lewis Leverton, Rector of this place
For fifty-three long years, warrants the Latin saw:
Domine dulcei decoram Domus tuae.
The world revolved, revolted and uprose
In carnage, destruction and renewal
Outside this hallowed spot, this placid cell,
While he performed his baptisms, gave communion,
Read long and abstract sermons, buried these his flock
Who lie about him now. Lieutenant-General Tuker
(Sir Francis Ivan Simon, to be sure),
K.C.I.E., C.B., with D.S.O. and O.B.E. –
Second King Edward the Seventh's Own Ghoorka Rifles,
Died in 1967. 'So he passed over, and all
The trumpets sounded for him on the other side.'
You smiled and wished him joy of his fanfare.
My favourite, though, is William Skewes, aged sixty,
Who, dying in 1866, minds all who pass of Job:
'Man dieth and wasteth away; yea, man giveth
Up the ghost, and where is he?'
These and their families live on, perhaps, in soil

46

About their graves, still tended faithfully,
Drifting amid the surging winds that move
The oaks and ilexes that overlook the coves
Below: a parish populated now by shades
Clustering about their church, their founder's shrine.
In this bright balmy light, celestial waves of sound
Arising from the sea to whisper to the soul,
The friendly presence of the past lives on,
Granting us benediction and respite
From heady and vainglorious pursuits of modern times.
Above the lych gate it is written thus:
'Da dhym yth-yu nessa dhe Dhew' –
Our old tongue speaks, that all shall hear and mark:
Good to me it is, near to my God.

June Evening, St Ervan

'Let me put on the lights,' the old lady said,
'Then you can see it all so much better.'
Nine o'clock and the rain plashed down
From ashes and sycamores arching the lane
Plunging down to the ford and holy well.
Tall as a man cow-parsley bloomed
And foxgloves reaching for light in that lush shade
Gleamed four feet high and higher as we passed
Under our streaming umbrellas, making for the church.

I remembered St Ervan from many years back:
A dim damp cell, the mildewed walls,
Musty pews and sweating slate-carved plates,
Memorials of gentry and farmers, the death's heads
Grinning upon the marble raised to one Ralph Keate.
The north chapel held a slate to William Arthur
And his wife: five sons, three daughters, stiffly knelt
In ruffs and breeches. And here they all were still,
Piously praying in this hidden retreat:
Now rather less neglected, almost glorified
By newly plastered walls and floor of polished blocks,
Red carpet laid upon it, and those cheerful lights.

Betjeman came here, was welcomed and then taught
By the rector, who tolled the bell, invited him,
A shy exploring youth, to tea. And lent
Him Machen's 'Secret Glory', opening out
The world of Celtic mysticism to his poet's mind.
A framed and scripted passage, taken from
'Summoned by Bells' hangs modestly
Upon the belfry wall, reminding visitors
And local worshippers of this,
St Ervan's claim to fame in literature.
And who indeed was Ervan? We may argue over him:

Obscure as Eval, Enodoc and Ewe. Erbyn, perhaps,
Father of Geraint, the King of Western Celts?
Or some forgotten namesake, hermit in these woods,
Sequestered from the mainstream of religious life,
The great works of the Age of Saints, who kept
His light of faith, and by example taught
The pagan Cornish all he knew of love?
'They blew up the tower a hundred years ago
With dynamite,' the verger said. 'A shocking state
'Twas in, and when St Issey tower was struck
By thunderbolt, that decided them.'
The two-stage stump is crowned with concrete now;
But three bells ring that had been silent here
A century.

The farming parish spreads beyond;
The schoolhouse now a residence, the Rectory
A hotel-restaurant; but at Trembleath, Farm of the Wolf,
The hay is in, the crops are reaching up
To slake their thirst in this relief of rain.
At Rumford agricultural engines throb,
Serviced and repaired, and haulage lorries roar
Their baleful ways along the country lanes
To building sites and refuse tips alike.
And by the church the modern village hall,
Heart of the parish social life, receives
The young, the old, the Women's Institute
And shields beneath its roof their simple honest joys.

There you and I went to a Cornish Evening once,
When Kernow Brass announced, with royal peal
On peal, their ringing marches – trumpet and trombone,
Cornet and euphonium – to our delighted ears.
And Hilda Bennett, clad in hat and wig,
With glasses falling off her nose, enacted out
A dialect story that convulsed us all
With aching merriment for helpless minutes then:
Bucolic humour at its ripest peak ...

'The chancel', said our guide, 'is crooked, if you will.
– Set at an angle to the nave, a fact
No one can quite explain.' I sign the book,
After the few names penned in June, and drop
Some money in the wall-box. 'We must go,
And you will want to lock up now.' The rain
Redoubles on the slate roof and the trees
Outside. 'Can we offer you a lift back home?'
– 'I like the walk, this time of evening, thank you.'
We left her musing in the silent chapel
By the slate memorials and the plaques.

Under our black and striped umbrellas we depart,
Along the lane with campion, vetch, herb Robert,
Hedge-bedstraw dripping fleering chains of light
As evening thickens, clamming in upon us.
Yet, as moisture seeps into my knees and feet
And even sheep find shelter in the hedge,
I hold that brave refurbishment, the will
Of those who will not let their church decay
In this unheeded corner of our land, aloft
In honour: guarding treasures of the past,
History's examples, faith of priest and flock,
A haven from the rage of modern life.

Hieroglyphics

'The world is certainly a great and stately volume of natural things;
and may be not improperly styled the hieroglyphics of a better.'
— William Penn.

Veryan bell-notes drift on rain-sown gusts
Across two miles of hedgerows, lanes and fields
To where the fulmars, daws and kittiwakes
Soar, contemptuous or oblivious of the drops
Hurtling down upon them: creatures of the spray,
Enjoying as I do the lash and wind,
Wet-footed yet exultant. Out beyond,
A solitary black-back swerves around Gull Rock
As Dodman disappears beneath a bank of cloud,
Its deluge hissing on the long sea-surge.
To stand above this plunging slope of cliff,
Staring at the tumult far below —
Wave clashing wave, the salt foam sluicing through
The deep-cleft gullies, reefs and fractured rocks;
As grey wings sail in effortless delight
Beneath, and pewter-purple glower
Of far-out surf meets dense and lowering cloud
In one gloom merging sea and sky the same;
As blackthorn stares with countless glistening eyes,
The bladder-campions waver in the gale
And blackbirds flute above the burning gorse —
These things combine to bring an elemental force
And pristine passion back to me again —
Scenes transient, ever-changing, changeless, bearing us
Forward from our own minute concerns, all drawing breath
From larger, deeper moods of nature: to a sense,
Eternal, never-failing, assuring blessedly —
Granted us in shadows and brief flashes
Above, within, below this protoplasmic scene.

Meditation on Three Churches of St Petroc

He came from Wales or Ireland, in his coracle,
A leathern boat with three or four disciples,
This prince who left his kingdom for a greater:
Struck water from the rock above Trebetherick shore,
Sent Samson out to preach. Assumed Lanwethinoc,
     Built ditches round its boundary,
     Stone crosses marked his sanctuary.
Then traversed Dumnonia, Armorica,
Founding churches, cells and lans. Cured palsy, banished
The last Cornish dragon to the sea. Padstow bears his name,
Though changed from Petrocstow. The tide that bore him here
Still flows in, never-failing, full as his own faith.

At Nanceventen, Valley Spring, the oracle
Would go to fast and pray; up to his neck
In river water he declaimed the psalms,
Sang hymns of praise to his beloved Creator.
He tamed a wolf to guard him whilst he slept;
     The hunted fawn protected,
     Warlike Constantine converted,
Sent west to end his days in solitude and prayer.
At Little Petherick, the church restored by Comper
Blazons in blue and gold the works the Abbot instituted.
Nanceventen bells chime out across the woods
He knew and loved, sustaining all his breath.

DW. (after P.Muna Trevenron)

The fertile bowl of Bodmin saw another miracle:
A table laid for him to feast on his arrival.
Guron departed; the second monastery was founded,
Soon to dominate the district. Prayer and work,
Protection of the poor and sick, the saint ordained.
      He rang his bell to end all slaveries
      Wherever it was heard. And centuries
After, manumissions in the medieval Gospels
Record his wishes. Franciscans, Benedictines,
Built their abbey churches, now defunct.
His church, cathedral of its see, continues strong
Where humbly he prepared for deathless death.

At Roche Rock

Pray for us, Gonandus, upon your Rock,
Pent in your eyrie above the ceaseless strife
And striving of a simple people to earn a simple living:
Gazing on this moorland prospect, giving
Grace to credulous worshippers, those whose life
Needs perpetual guidance, a shepherd to their flock.

Pray for us, hermit, leper, friend to all,
Fed by your daughter leaving cold morsels below
Where the ladder reaches the Chapel doorway, wind
Screaming or sighing about these chill walls: sinned
Against or sinning more we shall never know.
Still your knees imprint the harsh stone of your cell.

Pray for us, shrive us, grant us understanding
That we may emulate your holy poverty;
Turn from our clutter of prized possessions, things
Worthless in your eyes, baubles of mindless treasurings,
Towards that spiritual knowledge, a higher liberty:
Our finer urges and true destiny commanding.

Warleggan

The wind keens on Carburrow Tor,
Lamenting the great days of Bronze
When these rocky cairns were raised, tin-streaming
Carried on below, hut circles thatched with furze
Upon the downs. Later, miners drove in adits,
Altered watercourses, raised blowing-houses, stamps.
Wayside crosses marked church paths; the rabbits
Brought in by the Romans ate the meagre crops.
Iron Age camps grew bracken on the moor.
From Panter's bridge, Pont Yesu, pack-horse trains
Ascended to the ridge. Now beeches sway above the two-stage tower.
The Vicar, in his other parish, pulls the single bell.
Evensong at three: the organist reveals the power
Of his great instrument, their war memorial.
Two worshippers attend, two more than Densham had,
Who preached to cardboard figures, locked the parish out.
Ralph Tremur, the heretic, denied the Living Host;
Sam Gurney haunts the moorland roads about Trengoffe.
Two centuries ago the Faith was nearly lost;
Chapels raised the Spirit, this leaking church decayed.

We climb from Panter's Bridge, through oaks and withering elms,
The old road to the village, then beyond: the moors
Up to Carburrow, where crows and buzzards helm
The scourging air. Here larks in summer soar
And foxes roam the heaths by Deviock,
Treworder and Bofundle.
                    What in God's eye
Is Warleggan, poised above Bedalder's ferns?
The lonely bell calls us to prayer: the high
Trees move above us, bearing nests of rooks.
The candles of the faithful waver, yet burn on.

Carols on the Mount

(after a performance of 'Hail, Sacred Day' and other carols)

St Michael's Mount, the Cornish Mont St Michel –
Once owned by Norman Benedictines,
Our host, Lord St Levan, informs us,
Showing us round this island fortress,
Manor, palace, abbey, what you will.
Marazion, Penzance sprawl opposite; beyond them,
Ding Dong, Madron Moor, Godolphin Hill;
St Hilary spire stabs on the east
And the wide splinter of land pierces the sea
To the Lizard, across a pewter-sullen bay.

High in the Chapel we listen to carols,
Intricately woven, sung with precision, delicacy
(Although they're Cornish and should be shouted out
With primitive glee to tell the Saviour's birth).
The harp plucks melodies, variations and glissandi
From the soft December air. Michael himself, triumphant,
Cast in bronze, holds his sword cross-wise
Aloft, with Satan writhing, vanquished, underfoot.

'While Shepherds Watch' (from Treen) and 'Flaming Seraphs',
'Sans Day', 'A Virgin Most Pure', 'Shepherds Rejoice'
(from Padstow),
'A Child This Day is Born', 'The Angel Gabriel', and more –
Resound and intertwine their vivid harmonies;
Angelic solo voices rise and fall
Among the flags and treasuries.
I listen, all receiving,
Vibrating with such resonance and imports:
Intensified and brought to poignancy,
A spiritual embrace within this ringing canon –
Our inheritance of song, reborn

From simple earnest faithfulness and joy
Of foregone singers, now refined, arranged
By our composers in their modern styles.
Outside upon the turf above the rocks
The ancient granite cross from Celtic times
Heard other harps and voices, and the chants
Of medieval monks and precentors.
                                    So each age
Contributes in its own peculiar mode
Its disciplines of voice and melody,
All rising to enhance the Father's praise
With gratitude for Son and Spirit,
Hailing the Virgin, Shepherds, Cherubim
And Seraphim, Joseph and the Magi;
And all received, enshrined in ageless grace,
With equal value registered by Him
Upon the vast celestial scale:
Joining an eternal panoply of song
Expressing man's unceasing need to praise
His God and all Creation, until time
Is ended and eternity begun.

Keyne the Redhaired

Keyne, whose birth was wonderful
(Gwen of the Three Breasts, suckling triplets,
Gwethnok, Jacut and Winwallow,
Made a marvellous sight among men
But this was greater, passing that):
Your mother, caught in holy travail
Found her brimming bosom glowed
And sent out rays of light. Then,
With you an hour-old babe in her arms
She dreamed she nursed a dove ...

You who walked among our forests
By rushing waters meditating,
Who turned to stone the coiling snakes
On Glastonbury shore; whom people loved
With such devotion when they suffered you
Not to depart from *Carrek Luz en Cuz*,
Whilst you with smiling patience waited
Till the Word came down and silenced them,
Leading you abroad ...

Dear maid of the flashing eyes,
Who loved the tyrant's strong-armed son,
Yet, steadfast to your vows,
Refused his urgent pleas
And left our land with saddened heart:
First planting oak and Cornish elm,
Ash and willow round your Well,
And dedicating it to Marriage –
That other form of chastity, for those
Mere mortals who can never bear the flame,
The torch of holy love transfiguring you ...

O saint of fiery chastity
Whom men could love without desire,
Fearing in their hearts your shining vows,
The burning brand of your virginity –
Teach us, dear, to know your secret,
Beauty which subdues the flesh,
Lust fallen back, forgotten –
Passion shot to glory in Christ's love !

Carrek Luz en Cuz, the original Cornish name for St Michael's Mount, means Hoar Rock in the Wood. In St Keyne's time (6th Century A.D.) the Mount was in a forest, since submerged.

Carol Service at Trewen Church, Bodmin Moor

These our only stars, the flaring candles:
Scores, hundreds it seems, dipping and shooting,
Projecting a dance of light across the vaulted roof
And round the granite piers of this rude church,
Flouncing shadows on the fir and laurel
Decorations, led by the tall majestic cierges
On the small altar. The dreamy long-haired
Vicar drones his welcome, as though he's stepped
Out of his world of contemplation this brief hour.
The organist pedals the harmonium;
Her husband plays the clarinet; a violin and flute
Strike up, we launch into 'It Came Upon the Midnight Clear.'
Genesis Three, the woman tempting Adam:
'The Serpent shall go on his belly all his days.'
Then, 'Little Town of Bethlehem'; another lesson,
Micah, Five: 'Out of thee, O Bethlehem, shall come a Ruler.'
The Ladies' Circuit Choir, arrayed in blue, now sing
An anthem; leaning on my elbow, I am almost scorched
By a candle on the pew ledge. Outside now a dense
December mist closes us in
As if into the very hillside cave
Where shepherds and kings come seeking. Your cousin says
On Sunday afternoons the Vicar plays
Football at Lawhitton with the youngsters:
It does more good, he holds, than taking Evensong
At three p.m., as it belonged to be.
                              Times change,
New people come, but liven up the church,
This simple towerless structure on the Moor.
The clarinettist works for I.T.V.; the wife
(Who now sings solo, pulling out her stops)
Teaches music and conducts the choir.

'There was a man called John, sent to bear Witness
To the Light. And the Light was in the world,
But the world comprehended it not ...'
'*Adeste Fideles*' next, a stately sound:
'Yea, Lord, we greet Thee, born this happy morning.'
The holly and the ivy, they both are now full grown
Above the children's crib beside the Norman font.

Cups of tea and mince pies at the close,
As gleeful girls climb pews to douse the flames
Along the window ledges. Friends from scattered farms
Greet each other and enquire of families, relatives.
Electricity replaces candlelight,
The Mystery and the *Numen* vanishes.
So does the Vicar, back to slippers, hearth and books.
Treading between the pathside yews outside,
Presences darker than the night about them,

Past granite headstones to the iron gate,
We leave. No stars above. No light at all
Save for a lonely curtained cottage window,
And wavering headlamps of departing cars.
But all the way through muddy thorny lanes
To the wide curve of highway on the barren moor
The herald angels sing that Christ is born.

St Breock

An oven at Trevorder (long since gone)
Once held Tregagle's spirit, so they tell:
Lanhydrock Steward,
Duchy Receiver,
Through corruption he earned his own Hell.

St Breock holds no memorial to him:
His ghost howls on the Moor, bales Dozmary.
In this deep valley
Of ferns and lilies
Tregagle seems far enough away.

The village forebears all around are laid,
Pillars of trade in Wadebridge, farmers, hinds,
Beneath dark brooding yews
And slate-scrolled stones
Untroubled by upland winds.

The Stone of Waiting stands upon the Downs,
The high ridge-brow that dominates the scene.
Men Gortos, old as bronze:
What does it wait for? Us –
Or those who will one day rise again?

When Jan Tregagle is laid to rest at last,
Judgment indeed we all may know, in full.
The waiting over,
His crimes forgiven,
The Stone shall become his true memorial.

Jan Tregagle, the giant ghost of Bodmin Moor, is said to do penance for his sins by
baling out Dozmary Pool, using a limpet shell with a hole in it.

St-Breock

65

The Watchers at St Clement

The redshank steps lightly, delicately
On the mudbanks, prying and poking in the streams
Meandering from Tresillian bridge to Malpas.
Curlew, oystercatchers, teal, black-headed gulls;
Below the church, beyond the medieval quay
Constructed like a hedge of slate, immemorially
Standing the diurnal sweep and suck of tide,
The birdlife teems. And gathering naturalists gape,
Hold them in focus, fixing them on film,
Peering through high-powered telescopes and glasses.

In St Clement's church the organist
Practises for Sunday service: a voluntary of Bach's,
Cwm Rhondda, introit, quiet offertory.
The soft grey January afternoon forecloses
On lichened headstones in the graveyard,
Thatched roofs and minute plots, dead guelder roses;
A thrush sings loud against the darkening washes of the sky.
Here's the stone to Ignioc, a Roman magister
(Or merchant, maybe, or a Celtic chief
Educated by his conquerors: a Christian certainly):

Igniocus Vilatus Filius Torrici, with Ogam marks
And rough Greek cross; fifth century A.D.
Did he pace this river walk and see such life
Swarming and swooping on the creek, from dense oak woods
To reed beds and lagoons? Was he worried
Where to hide his ancient Roman coins?
Doubtless he regulated trade and oversaw
The export of streamed tin brought from the moors
For Brittany and beyond.

                The shelduck preen
And scoop the mud; their umber wings
And gloss-green heads appearing ebony
As one by one they take to flight and whirr
Above the trees before the flooding tide
Which creeps and seeps and sluices silently,
Shrinking the mudflats and the saltgrass isles.
A shag comes skimming blackly past us, seeking
Small fry nosing out upon the rise. Herons
Stand in silent vigil in the flow, spearing
With swift sure merciless plunge the eels
Or mullet swimming unsuspectingly among their legs;
And in the pond by Menadews a blue electric bolt,
The kingfisher, flames above the mallards and the grebes.

Lights appear in cottages, and woodsmoke curls
Above the roofs. The thrush is silent now;
The organist locks up and paces home,
Clicks the oak lych-gate beneath the Parish Room.
The tide is full, the trees one shadowed mass;
The thin curved moon, a silver scimitar,
Is rising over Roseland. Birds are hushed;
Hardly a rook to rend the twilit peace.
The watchers change their boots and pack away
Their cameras, meters and binoculars,
Depart in cars to other, busier parts.
O glorious silent surge of water on the bank,
And luminous calm of evening on the strand !
The shades of Ignioc and early worshippers
Now drift and dream beneath the Angevin tower
And, watching over their hallowed heritage,
Protect this village life for one more night.

In the 18th Century, a hoard of Roman coins was found across the river from
St Clement, most of them of the period of Gallienus (Emperor 253-268 A.D.).

St John's Methodist Church, Padstow
1827-1987

It stood here, where the bland grey tarmac
(Private Car Park Only) is washed by rains, and yawns,
An accusing space left in the centre of our town.
I recall it well enough, having been baptised here
And sent to Sunday School in the Hall next door,
Until, at the age of four, there was a row –
A disagreement, misunderstanding perhaps, some insult
Construed, as happens in small places;
And I was sent to Sunday School 'up Church'.
Over the years there have been weddings and funerals,
Mainly those of aunts and uncles and cousins,
All good Wesleyans, or nominally so. Uncle Will,
Who built boats in his backyard on the hill
That never got to sea, was Chapel, certainly,

Though never setting foot in here for years; and so was Uncle Matt,
Known in his time as a Revolutionary Red (A Radical
Liberal, actually) – who once proposed
The harbour should be filled in for a car park.
Aunt Amy fell out with this one and that, was always late
For service (a family failing, I admit), but very staunch:
In later years, retired from teaching school,
A loyal member of the Sisterhood.
                              The golden oak of benches
And smell of polish lovingly applied; the sunlight
Flooding through the coloured glass, the airy warm
Feeling as the choir filtered into the gallery
Beginning the Introit, the organ humming soft,
And then the congregation bursting forth
In joyful song that put to shame
Our half-hearted hymning up to Church:
        'O for a thousand tongues to sing
        My blest Redeemer's praise:
        The glories of my God and King,
        The triumphs of his grace!'
Memorials fixed to walls told of the elders
Who, prospering more than most, endowed the place.
The preachers would appear and tell us straight
How we had sinned, and sinned again,
But must return to His redeeming love.
At Harvest Festival the corn and bread and fruit
Bulged the tables, overflowed the pulpit and the rails.
Each family had its own appointed pew,
Though latterly the place was seldom filled.

I thought they were a narrow lot, those people,
Kindly enough but disapproving of too much,
Especially drink and gambling. Now I think
They knew what they were saying then, to judge
By what goes on around us. We could do
With a decent Revival here today,

70

And a bellyful of hell-fire preaching too.
But, having demolished our chapel (its roof
Was pitched too low, the walls pushed out –
It couldn't be saved, they say), how can we hope
For such a thing in this tourist trap today?
And what would John and Charles, those doughty horsemen,
Out in all weathers, preaching to fishermen and miners,
Think of the car park now marking the spot,
Bringing the few still faithful here on Sunday
To the new plush Church they've built next door?

Three Churches by the Water

St Michael, Porthilly

Porthilly, Salty Landing Place, I have known
From early childhood; we came to it across
The Camel, by ferry then, each summer,
And later in our own boat, landing beside the church
At high tide: to view the long-loved, well-remembered
Graveyard with its slate hedge bounding the tide;
The single bell in the little tower would sound
Its steady plaintive note across the estuary.
We passed the great wheel-head of the granite cross
By the porch (which my friend Gwas Gwethnok
Would insist belongs to the mighty shaft
In Padstow churchyard). Inside we felt the cool
Damp air upon our burning legs and faces;
Then stood and read those simple slate memorials.
     'Gently, softly, silent tread
     In the region of the dead.
     Here and there behold a friend:
     Mortal, view thy certain end.'

St Winnow

Is different, across the muddy strands
Of the Fowey below Lostwithiel, from Lantyan,
Once the palace of King Mark (if Béroul
In his Tristan poem was right).
Birds at evening cheeping, chittering, shrieking, croaking
From that ancestral woodland, raise in us
Memories of that angry Cornish king, and those star-crossed,
        romance-doomed lovers,
Tristan his son, and his own chosen bride,
Iseult of Ireland.
                    Inside the church
The piper on the medieval bench-end
Plays on, droning that eternal tragedy.

St Just in Roseland

Peace-betided creek, haven of Geraint,
King of Dumnonia, last of Arthur's captains
To rally his Celts and stand against the Saxons
At Dyrham, fourteen centuries ago . . .
Here's commemorated Jestyn, his son,
A hermit who did not inherit the throne,
Fasting and meditating in this holy vale –
His well still flows from the churchyard path,
Is used for baptisms today.
                         A regal
Blessed spot, where under the swan-necked tower
A tropic garden grows: rhododendrons, palms,
Magnolias, lilies, which becalm our restless times;
Jewel of the Roseland, haven for all who find it:
Glen of royal benediction for all time.

The Silence at Come-to-Good

O clear and undivided is the Word we seek,
Rising from the Silence of the faithful few.
Clear and undivided is the knowledge of the Lord
When meeting here we listen for His still small voice.
Under this high thatched havening roof the Friends
Come to a greater good than others know.
Curious explorers seeking the picturesque
Find in this quiet lane beside a farm
A sudden well of peace, a witness to their Faith
Who in the past withstood the scorn, the lash
Of Puritanic laws, incarceration for their pleas:
George Fox and Loveday Hambly, Ann Upcott...

O hallowed Come-to-Good, or *Cwm-ty-quite*,
Valley of the House in the Woods: it comes to this,
That humankind must seek Him as it can,
In myriad ways, in song and prayer and thought,

In Eucharist and sermon, confession, holy books...
Yet the kernel of all faith is surely silence.
Until the world is shut out, and the fog
Of its coarse pleasures can recede, we cannot hear:
Until we bow in quietude and thrust all words
And argument away, we never shall receive
The Logos latent in our inmost souls.

O clear and undivided is the Word
That rises from the silence of these few.

George Fox, the Quaker leader, was imprisoned in 1655 in the infamous dungeon
of Doomsday, Launceston Castle, for publishing a manifesto. Loveday Hambly of
Tregongreeves was also imprisoned for her beliefs. Ann Upcott of
St Austell was put in the stocks for mending a garment on Sunday. Many other
Quakers were fined for not attending church, refusing to pay tithes, etc.